This Journal Belongs To:

Be creative!
Write about everything
you see, hear or eat.
Start with a title.
Make it visual by drawing
or adding stickers
to the picture box.
Most of all, have fun!

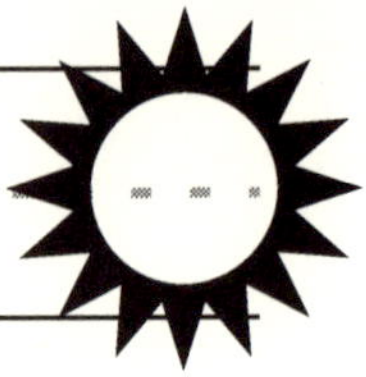

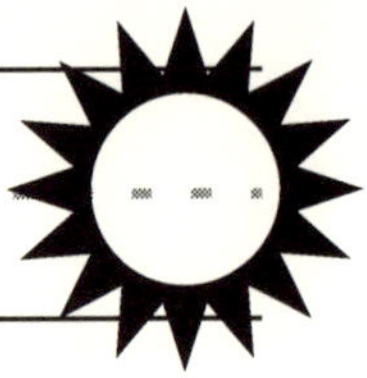

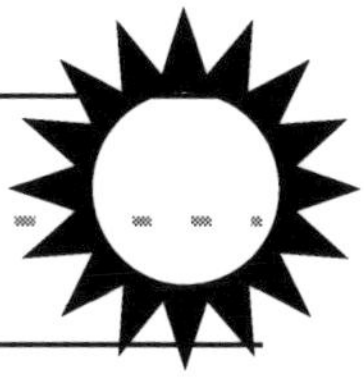

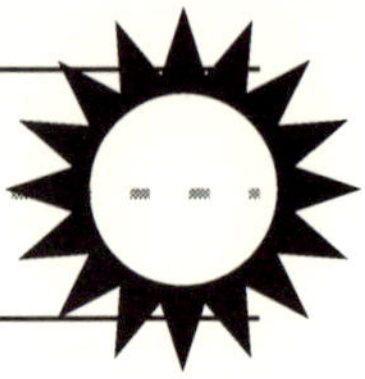

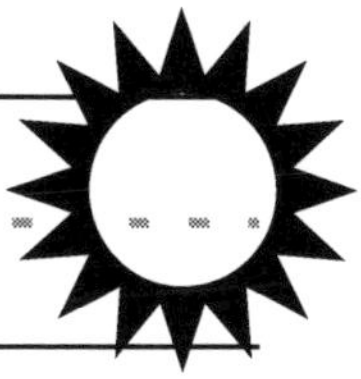

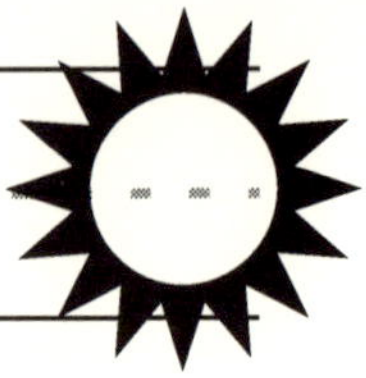

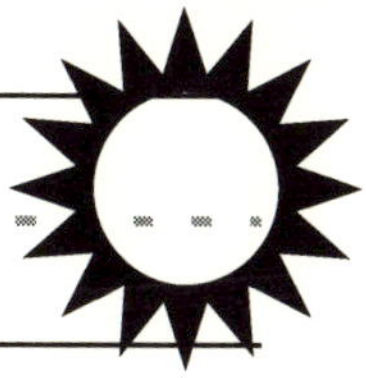

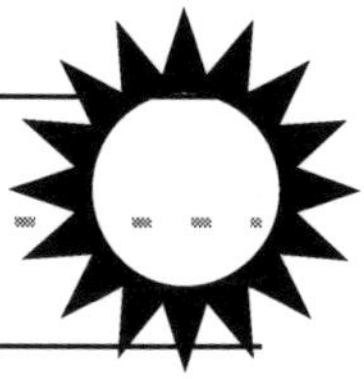

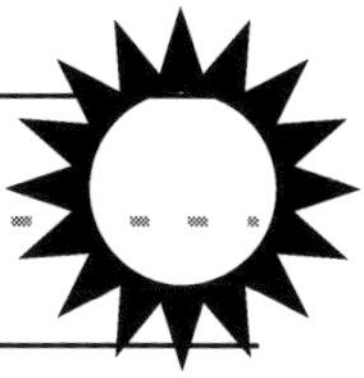

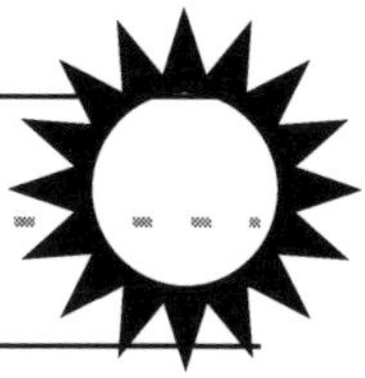

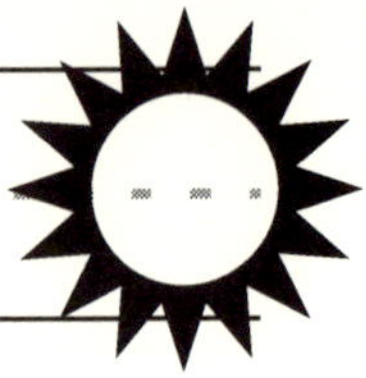

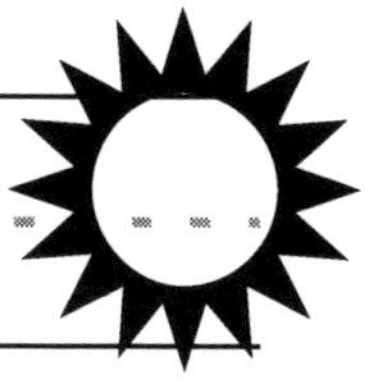

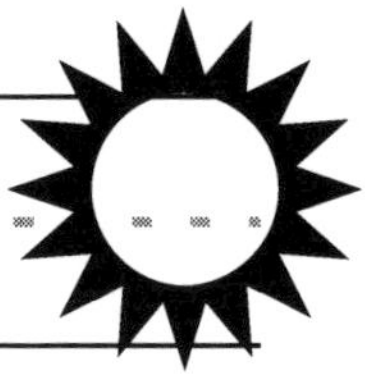

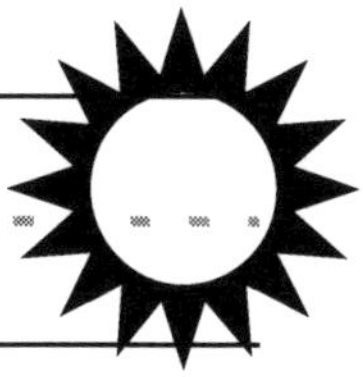

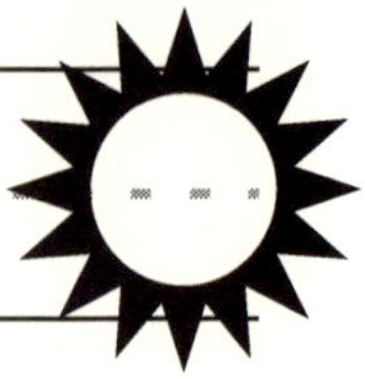

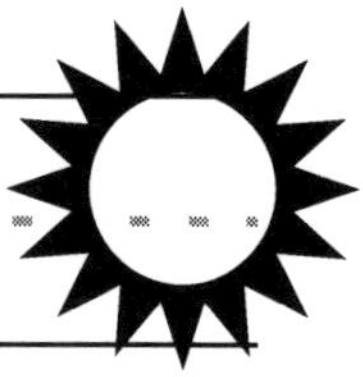

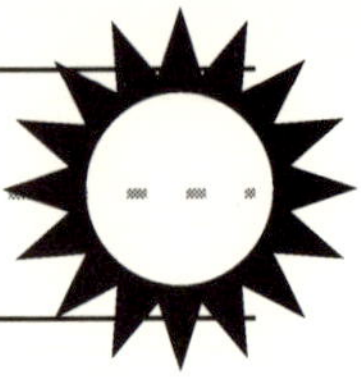

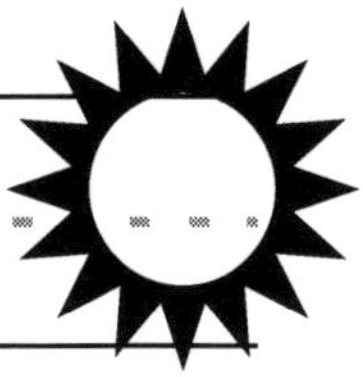

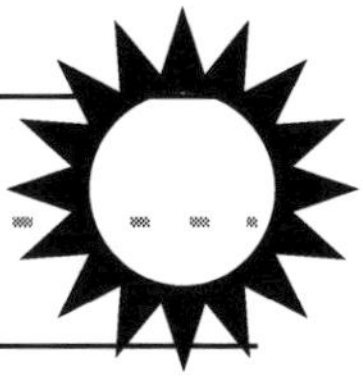

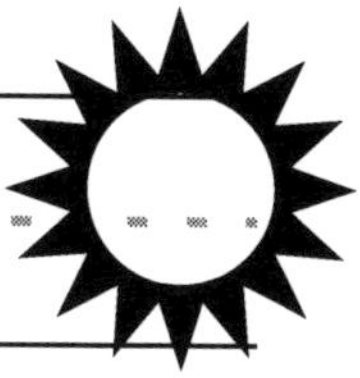

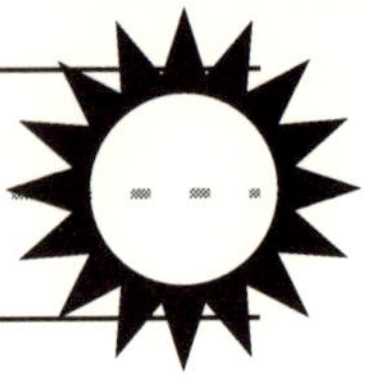

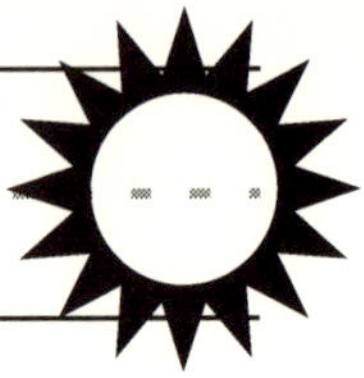

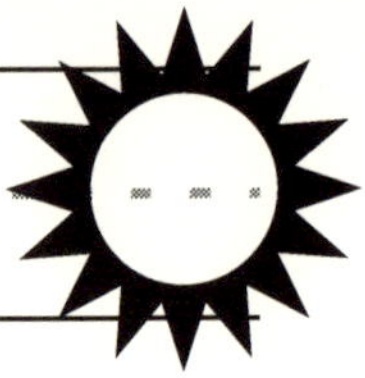

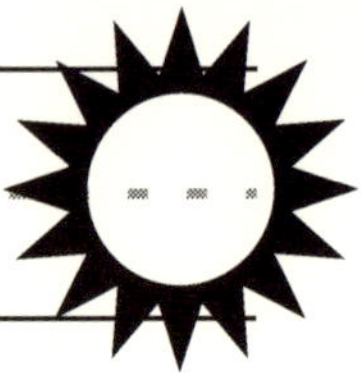

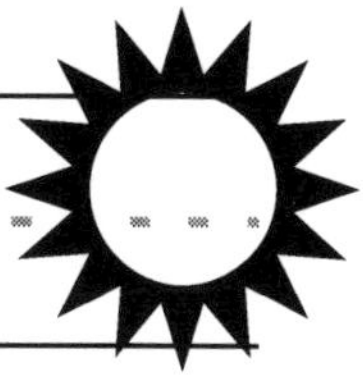

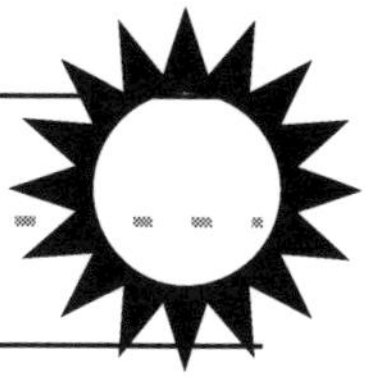

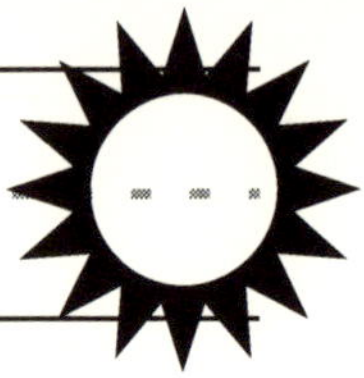

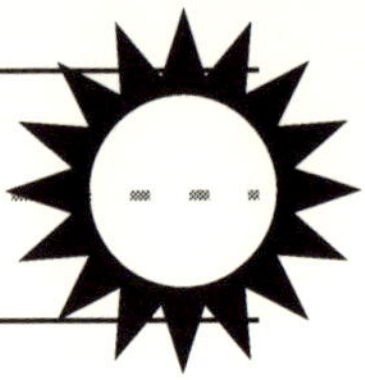

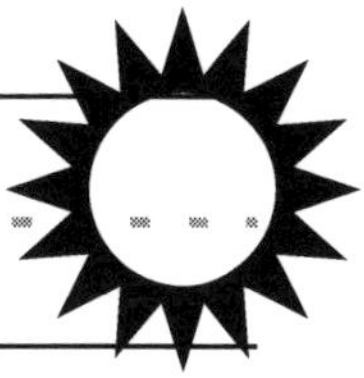

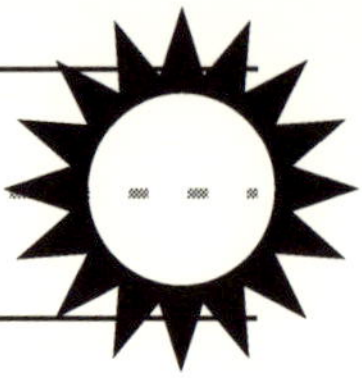

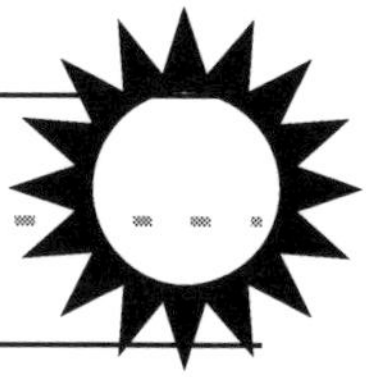

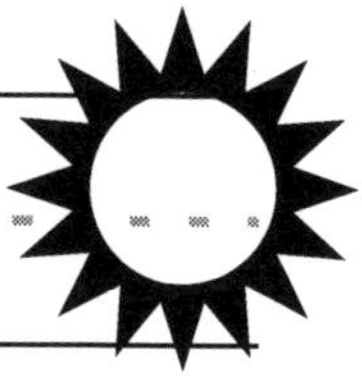

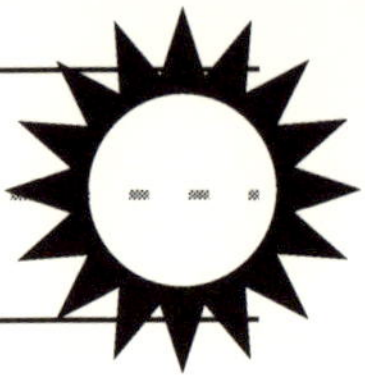

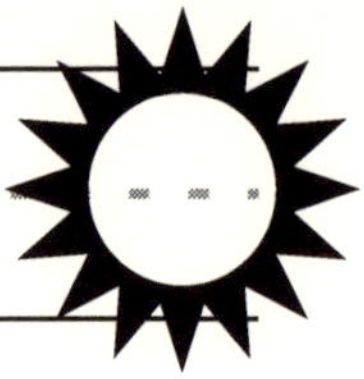

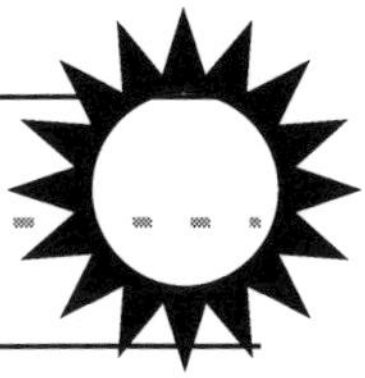

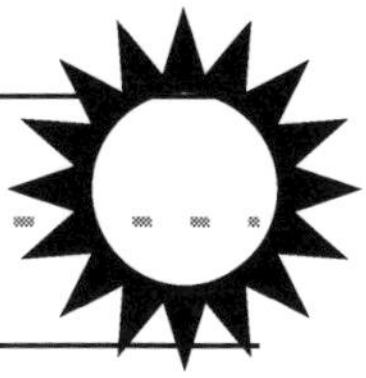

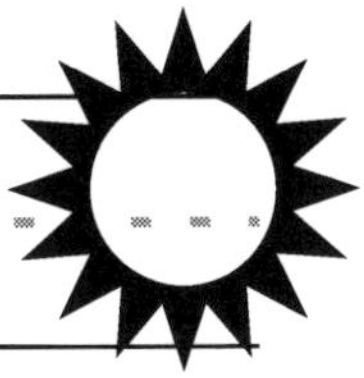

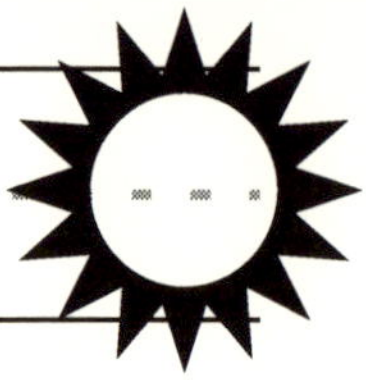

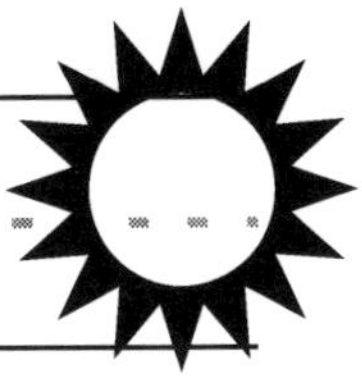

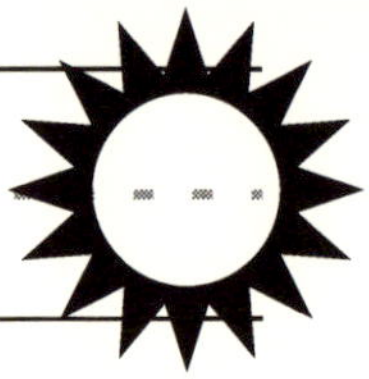

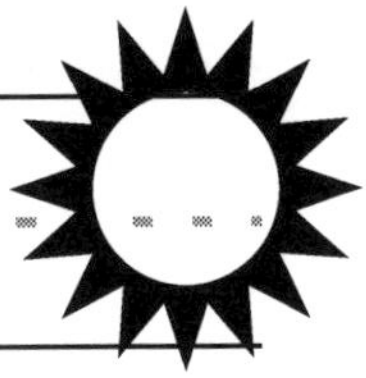

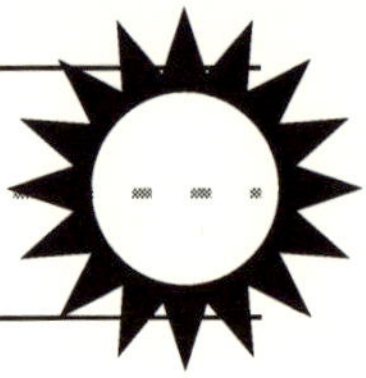

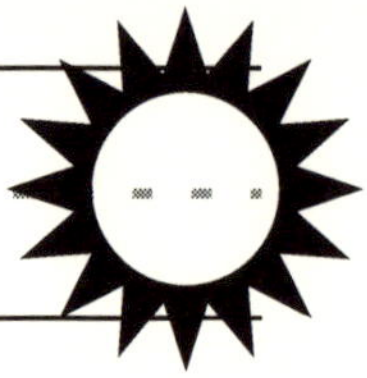

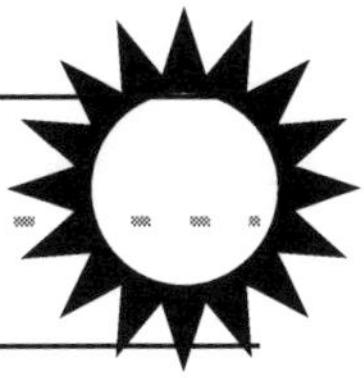

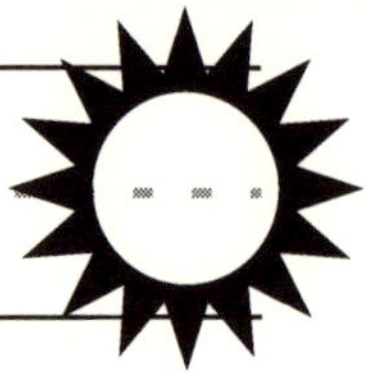

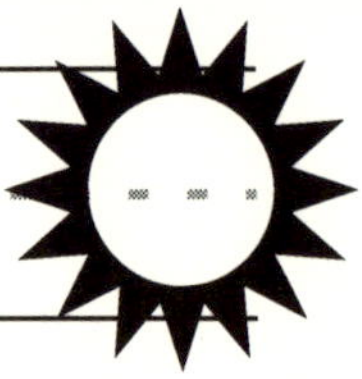

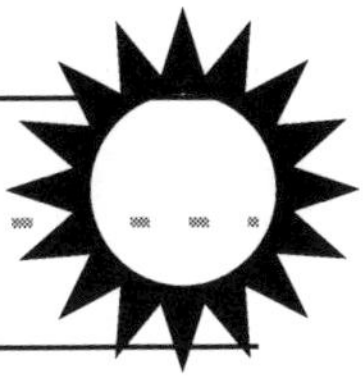